SOCCER STARS

# JULIE
# ERTZ

**BENJAMIN BURDETT**

**PowerKiDS** press™

New York

Published in 2019 by The Rosen Publishing Group, Inc.
29 East 21st Street, New York, NY 10010

First Edition

Editor: Elizabeth Krajnik
Book Design: Michael Flynn

Photo Credits: Cover (Ertz), p. 1 Kevin C. Cox/Getty Images Sport/Getty Images; cover (stadium background) winui/Shutterstock.com; cover (player glow) Nejron Photo/Shutterstock.com; pp. 3, 23, 24 (background) Narong Jongsirikul/Shutterstock.com; pp. 4, 6–8, 10, 12, 14, 16, 18–20, 22 (ball background) DRN Studio/Shutterstock.com; p. 5 Manuel Queimadelos Alonso/Bongarts/Getty Images; p. 6 Alex Menendez/AP Images; p. 7 Joe Petro/Icon Sportswire/AP Images; p. 8 JRyder1/Shutterstock.com; p. 9 Bill Janscha/AP Images; p. 10 Renan Teuman/Shutterstock.com; p. 11 Chris Graythen/Getty Images Sport/Getty Images; p. 13 Daiju Kitamura/AFLO SPORT/Alamy; p. 15 Mike Ehrmann/Getty Images Sport/Getty Images; p. 17 Tony Quinn/Icon Sportswire/Getty Images; p. 18 Mike Hewitt/FIFA/Getty Images; p. 19 Maddie Meyer/FIFA/Getty Images; p. 21 Celso Junior/Getty Images Sport/Getty Images; p. 22 Jonathan Daniel/Getty Images Sport/Getty Images.

Cataloging-in-Publication Data

Names: Burdett, Benjamin.
Title: Julie Ertz / Benjamin Burdett.
Description: New York : PowerKids Press, 2019. | Series: Soccer stars | Includes glossary and index.
Identifiers: ISBN 9781538345047 (pbk.) | ISBN 9781538343494 (library bound) | ISBN 9781538345054 (6 pack)
Subjects: LCSH: Ertz, Julie, 1992–Juvenile literature. | Women soccer players–United States–Biography–Juvenile literature. | Soccer–United States–History–Juvenile literature.
Classification: LCC GV942.7.E789 B883 2019 | DDC 796.334092 B–dc23

Manufactured in the United States of America

CPSIA Compliance Information: Batch #CWPK19 For Further Information contact Rosen Publishing, New York, New York at 1-800-237-9932

# CONTENTS

# THE EARLY DAYS

Julie Ertz (**née** Johnston) was born to Kristi and David Johnston on April 6, 1992, in Mesa, Arizona. Julie and her sister, Melanie, played club soccer for the Arizona Arsenal Soccer Club, which used to be known as the Gilbert Soccer Club.

In 2004, Julie and Melanie switched teams to play for Sereno Soccer Club in Phoenix. They wanted to play on a more **competitive** team. Their mother drove them an hour each way for practice until Julie was old enough to drive. Playing for Sereno helped Julie become the star **athlete** she is today. She said, "[switching to Sereno] ended up being the best decision I've ever made."

## STAR POWER

In many countries around the world, people call soccer "football." In countries such as the United States and Australia, the sport is called "soccer" because there's another sport called "football."

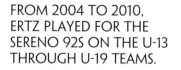

FROM 2004 TO 2010,
ERTZ PLAYED FOR THE
SERENO 92S ON THE U-13
THROUGH U-19 TEAMS.

# GOALS AND GRADES

From 2006 to 2010, Ertz attended Dobson High School in Mesa. She chose not to play for her school soccer team. Instead, Ertz spent her time playing for Sereno. She played whichever position the coaches wanted her to play and she was comfortable playing anywhere. Ertz was named captain of her team and helped them win nine state **championships**.

CONNECTING WITH HER FANS HAS ALWAYS BEEN IMPORTANT TO ERTZ.

Ertz's success wouldn't have been possible if she hadn't worked hard in school. She was a member of the National Junior Honor Society and the National Honor Society. For all four years at Dobson, Ertz volunteered as a student athletic trainer.

# MONEY HURTS

Even though Ertz was a talented player, she had to work hard for all her successes. When she was 13 years old, her parents sat her down to make sure she was serious about playing. Playing on a club team was expensive, and her family didn't have much money. She told her parents that she wanted to keep playing, so they continued to support her.

Ertz went to Santa Clara University, an expensive private school in California, even though she had only been searching for schools that offered full-ride **scholarships**. Luckily, she earned a full-ride scholarship at the end of her first season.

**SOCCER FIELD AT SANTA CLARA UNIVERSITY**

ERTZ WAS SCARED SHE WOULDN'T BE ABLE TO AFFORD GOING TO SCHOOL AT SANTA CLARA AND WOULD HAVE TO GO TO A DIFFERENT COLLEGE. HER COACH, JERRY SMITH, DIDN'T WANT TO LOSE SUCH A GREAT PLAYER SO HE FOUND A WAY TO KEEP HER ON THE TEAM.

**JERRY SMITH**

# BUCKING LIKE A BRONCO

In 2010, Ertz joined the Santa Clara Broncos. She played as a defender, a midfielder, and a forward for the team. Ertz was named the West Coast Conference **Freshman** of the Year. During her sophomore, or second, year, Ertz was a 2011 M.A.C. Hermann Trophy semi-finalist.

Her junior, or third, year, Ertz was voted U.S. Soccer Young Female Player of the Year. As a **senior**, Ertz was named West Coast Conference Player of the Year. Throughout her college **career**, Ertz was a starter for 58 of the 59 games she played. She scored 29 goals and had 18 **assists** for a total of 76 points.

ERTZ WAS A FIRST TEAM ALL-AMERICAN PLAYER IN 2011, 2012, AND 2013. SHE WAS ALSO NAMED TO THE ALL-WCC FIRST TEAM IN 2011, 2012, AND 2013.

# ON THE WORLD STAGE

In 2012, Ertz also played **international** U-20 youth soccer for the U.S. women's national team (WNT). Ertz's teammates named her captain and she took her leadership role seriously. The team played 13 international matches, and Ertz helped them go to the 2012 FIFA U-20 Women's World Cup in Japan. On the road to the World Cup, Ertz played in all 13 matches and scored four goals.

On September 8, 2012, the U.S. WNT defeated Germany 1–0 for their third-ever World Cup win. Ertz, a defender, won the Bronze Ball as the tournament's third-best player. She was also named the 2012 U.S. Soccer Young Female Player of the Year.

## STAR POWER

According to FIFA, the earliest form of soccer can be traced back to a Chinese game known as *cuju*, which became popular during the Han Dynasty (206 BC to AD 220).

THE BRONZE BALL IS AWARDED TO THE THIRD-BEST PLAYER AT THE FULL NATIONAL LEVEL AS WELL AS THE U-20 LEVEL.

# FAMILY MATTERS

Playing soccer in college set the stage for Ertz to become a world-famous player, but her time in California was important for another reason, too. When Julie was a sophomore, she went to a Stanford baseball game. Zach Ertz, a junior football player for Stanford, was with his friends and decided to go meet her.

Even though the two went to different schools and didn't have much spare time due to playing sports, they made it work. They got engaged on February 26, 2016, and they were married on March 26, 2017, in Goleta, California. Zach says they're "each other's Number One fan and supporter."

## STAR POWER

Ertz not only married an athlete, but grew up around them, too. Her sister, Melanie, played soccer at Grand Canyon University and her father played football at Louisiana State.

ZACH ERTZ IS A FORMER STANFORD ALL-AMERICAN AND TIGHT END FOR THE NFL'S PHILADELPHIA EAGLES.

# BECOMING A PRO

On January 17, 2014, the Chicago Red Stars selected Ertz as the third overall pick in the first round of the 2014 National Women's Soccer League College **Draft**. On April 19, 2014, Ertz made her first **professional** appearance against the Western New York Flash as a defender. She was named the 2014 NWSL **Rookie** of the Year.

During the 2015 season, Ertz played in 11 games for a total of 990 minutes. The team made it to the playoffs, but they lost to FC Kansas City. Ertz was named to the NWSL Best XI. During the 2016 season, Ertz played in 12 games for a total of 1,080 minutes.

IN 2017, ERTZ PLAYED IN 22 GAMES FOR A TOTAL OF 1,932 MINUTES AND SCORED FOUR GOALS AS A MIDFIELDER. SHE WAS NAMED TO THE NWSL SECOND XI.

# WORLD CUP WINNERS

In January 2013, Ertz was called up to the senior national team to play as a defender. In 2014, Ertz played as a midfielder. Just one day before the WNT played its first match of the 2014 CONCACAF Women's Qualifying tournament, Ertz was added to the roster to take the place of an injured teammate. On October 24, 2014, the U.S. WNT beat Mexico in the semi-finals to qualify for the 2015 FIFA Women's World Cup.

AFTER WINNING THE WOMEN'S WORLD CUP, THE TEAM WENT ON A 10-GAME VICTORY TOUR FROM AUGUST 16, 2015, IN PITTSBURGH, PENNSYLVANIA, TO DECEMBER 16, 2015, IN NEW ORLEANS, LOUISIANA, TO CELEBRATE THE UNITED STATES' THIRD WOMEN'S WORLD CUP TITLE.

On April 14, 2015, the U.S. WNT's head coach announced the 23 players who would represent the United States at the FIFA Women's World Cup. Ertz was selected to play as a defender in her first Women's World Cup. On July 5, 2015, the U.S. WNT won against Japan in the final.

## STAR POWER

Ertz was chosen as one of 23 players of the 2015 FIFA Women's World Cup All-Star team. Four other U.S. WNT players were chosen to play on the team: Hope Solo, Meghan Klingenberg, Megan Rapinoe, and Carli Lloyd.

# THE ROAD TO RIO

On January 26, 2016, the U.S. WNT's head coach named Ertz to the 20-player roster for the 2016 CONCACAF Women's Olympic Qualifying Championship. The WNT got its ticket to the 2016 Summer Olympics in Rio de Janeiro, Brazil, after a 5–0 win against Trinidad and Tobago in the semifinal.

On July 12, 2016, the U.S. WNT's head coach named Ertz to the 18-player roster for the 2016 Summer Olympics. Ertz was chosen to play as a defender. This marked her first appearance on the U.S. Olympic Team. Team USA lost to Sweden in the quarterfinals on August 12, 2016.

## STAR POWER

On February 21, 2016, the WNT beat Canada 2–0 to win the CONCACAF Olympic Qualifying Championship. This win marked the fourth time in a row the U.S. WNT won the championship.

TEAM USA WON GOLD MEDALS IN ATLANTA, GEORGIA (1996), ATHENS, GREECE (2004), BEIJING, CHINA (2008), AND LONDON, ENGLAND (2012). THE TEAM ALSO WON SILVER IN SYDNEY, AUSTRALIA, IN 2000.

# ANYTHING IS POSSIBLE

Ertz was named the 2017 U.S. Soccer Female Player of the Year. She is the third-ever player to be named both the U.S. Soccer Female Player of the Year and Young Female Player of the Year.

In 2015, after winning the Women's World Cup, the WNT was honored at the White House. In his speech, President Barack Obama said, "Playing like a girl means being the best." Ertz and her teammates' successes continue to **inspire** many young soccer players to chase their dreams and be the best they can be. Go Julie!

# GLOSSARY

**assist:** The action of a player who makes it possible for a teammate to score a goal.

**athlete:** A person who is trained in or good at sports, games, or exercises that require physical skill and strength.

**career:** A period of time spent doing a job or activity.

**championship:** A contest to find out who's the best player or team in a sport.

**competitive:** Characterized by or based on a situation in which more than one person or team is striving for the same thing.

**draft:** The practice of choosing someone to play on a professional sports team.

**freshman:** A student in the first year of high school or college.

**inspire:** To move someone to do something great.

**international:** Occurring between nations.

**née:** Used after a married woman's last name to identify the last name she had when she was born.

**professional:** Taking part in a sport to make money.

**rookie:** A first-year player in a professional sport.

**scholarship:** Money a school or organization gives to help a student pay for their education.

**senior:** A student in the final year of high school or college. Also, higher in standing or rank than another person or team in the same position.

# INDEX

# WEBSITES

Due to the changing nature of Internet links, PowerKids Press has developed an online list of websites related to the subject of this book. This site is updated regularly. Please use this link to access the list:
www.powerkidslinks.com/socstars/ertz